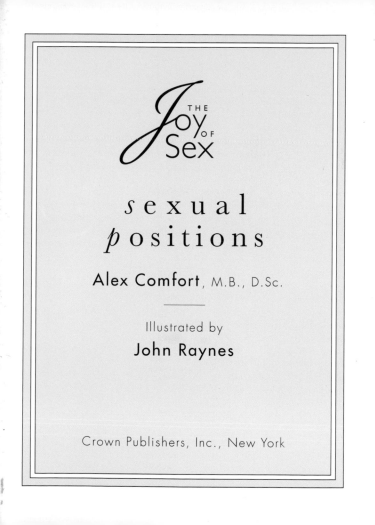

The Joy of Sex

sexual positions

Alex Comfort, M.B., D.Sc.

Illustrated by
John Raynes

Crown Publishers, Inc., New York

The JOY OF SEX ® Series

Copyright © 1997 by Mitchell Beazley

All rights reserved. No part of this book may be reproduced or transmitted
in any form or by any means, electronic or mechanical, including
photocopying, recording, or by any information storage and retrieval
system, without permission in writing from the publisher.

Published by Crown Publishers, New York,
New York. Member of the Crown Publishing Group,
a division of Random House, Inc.

www.randomhouse.com

CROWN is a trademark and the Crown colophon is
a registered trademark of Random House, Inc.

Printed in Hong Kong

Library of Congress Cataloging-in-Publication Data

is available on request.

ISBN 0-609-60033-8

10 9 8 7 6 5 4 3 2

First American Edition

Material in this book excerpted from *The Joy of Sex*

c o n t e n t s

i n t r o d u c t i o n

ex and its enjoyment is a seamless whole, but within its richness some themes arouse particular delight and encourage lovers to experiment. The almost infinite variety of sexual positions is one area where many couples are eager to explore, and this 'pillow book', *Sexual Positions*, is intended for them. The book includes a number of positions for making love that have been tried over the centuries in different cultures, with the objective the total enjoyment of sex. It does not treat the exciting richness of sexual positions as a detached exercise in athletics, though that is fulfilling for some; it makes a point, rather, of emphasizing the roles of love, tenderness and fidelity in a truly fulfilling physical relationship.

Although authors of books about sex have been assiduous collectors of positions, there is, in fact, little evidence that one position is better than any other — unless, like the Indian eroticians, you aim to combine sex with yoga. Yet there is a case for having a range of postures, both for variety and because many couples find that some really do suit them better than others. Also, reading the possibilities, singly, or as a couple, is exciting and suggests new possibilities.

Lovers will find that they settle down over time to a few positions, the common matrimonial being the most popular and one of the women-on-top the next. Don't expect 57 varieties alone to work wonders, but it's worth keeping them handy for a rainy day, or when you think things are getting dull – if ever they do.

Men and women show a truly remarkable adaptability in body size. We say: try anything you like, and drop what you don't like. These positions have been selected to stimulate the young and the not-so-young. But for most couples of all ages, shapes and sizes, its the doing rather than the description that counts. Read on . . . and enjoy.

Alex Comfort M.B., D.Sc.

love

We use the same word for man—woman, mother—child, child—parent, and I—mankind relations — rightly, because they are a continuous spectrum. In talking about sexual relations, it seems right to apply it to any relationship in which there is mutual tenderness, respect and consideration — from a total interdependence where the death of one

6

maims the other for years, to an agreeable night together. The intergrades are all love, all worthy, all part of human experience.

Some meet the needs of one person, some of another – or of the same person at different times. That's really the big problem of sexual ethics, and it's basically a problem of self-understanding and of communication. You can't assume that your 'conditions of love' are applicable to, or accepted by, any other party; you can't assume that these won't be changed quite unpredictably in both of you by the experience of loving; you can't necessarily know your own mind.

love . . . *the essential openness of a real relationship between people* . . .

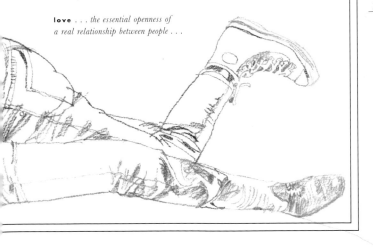

f sexual love can be – and it is – the supreme human experience, it must be also a bit hazardous. It can give us our best and our worst moments. In this respect it's like mountain climbing – over-timid people miss the whole experience; reasonably balanced and hardy people accept the risks for the rewards, but realize that there's a difference between this and being foolhardy. Love, moreover, involves someone else's neck beside your own. At least you can make as sure as may be that you don't exploit or injure someone. Getting them to sign a form of consent before they start isn't the answer either. There was a hell of a lot to be said for the English Victorian idea of not being a cad ('person devoid of finer or gentlemanly feelings'). A cad can be of either sex.

Marriage between two rival actor-managers, each trying to produce the other regardless, isn't love. The relationship between a prostitute and a casual client where, for reasons they don't quite get, real tenderness and respect occur, is.

love *A potentially overwhelming experience
worth all the risks*

t e n d e r n e s s

enderness doesn't exclude extremely violent games (though many people neither need nor want these), but it does exclude clumsiness, heavy handedness, lack of feedback, spitefulness and non-rapport generally, shown fully in the way you touch each other. What it implies at root is a constant awareness of what your partner is feeling, plus the knowledge of how to heighten that feeling, gently, toughly, slowly or fast, and this only comes from an inner state of mind between you. No really tender person can just turn over and go to sleep.

Many if not most inexperienced men, and some women, are just naturally clumsy – either through haste, through anxiety, or through lack of sensing how the other sex feels. Men in general are harder-skinned than women – don't grab breasts, stick fingers

tenderness *What it implies is a constant awareness of what your partner is feeling*

11

tenderness *Gently does it can be
exciting for both of you*

into the vagina, handle female skin as if it was your own, or (and
this goes for both sexes) misplace bony parts of your anatomy.
More girls respond to very light than to very heavy stimulation –
just brushing pubic hair or skin hairs will usually do far more than
a whole-hand grab. At the same time don't be frightened – neither of you is made of glass. Women by contrast often fail to use
enough pressure, especially in handwork, though the light, light
variety is a sensation on its own. Start very gently, making full use
of the skin surface, and work up. Stimulus toleration in any case
increases with sexual excitement until even hard blows can
become excitants (though not for everyone). This loss of pain

sense disappears almost instantly with orgasm, so don't go on too long, and be extra gentle as soon as he or she has come.

If you are really heavy-handed, a little practice with inanimate surfaces, dress-fastenings and so on will help. Male strength is a turn-on in sex, but it isn't expressed in clumsy handwork, bear-hugs and brute force – at least not as starters. If there is a problem here, remember you both can talk. Few people want to be in bed on any terms with a person who isn't basically tender, and most people are delighted to be in bed with the right person who is. The ultimate test is whether you can bear to find the person there when you wake up. If you are actually pleased, then you're onto the right thing.

f i d e l i t y

idelity, infidelity, jealousy and so on. We've deliber-
ately not gone into the ethics of lifestyle. The facts are that
few men and slightly more women in our culture go through life
with sexual experience confined to one partner only. What suits
a particular couple depends on their needs, situation, anxieties
and so on. These needs are a particularly delicate problem in
communication: if mutual comprehension is complete and ongo-
ing you can count yourselves lucky. Active deception always hurts
a relationship. Complete frankness which is aimed to avoid guilt
or as an act of aggression against a partner can do the same.
The real problem arises from the fact that sexual relations can be
anything for different people on different occasions, from a game
to a total fusion of identities; the heartaches arise when each

fidelity *In a relationship this means that you know
where each of you stands*

partner sees it differently. There is no sexual relationship which doesn't involve responsibility, because there are two or more people involved: anything which, as it were, militantly excludes a partner is hurtful, yet to be whole people we have at some point to avoid total fusion with each other – 'I am I and you are you, and neither of us is on earth to live up to the other's expectations.' People who communicate sexually have to find their own fidelities. All we can suggest is that you discuss them so that at least you know where each of you stands.

fidelity *All relationships involve responsibility
to yourself and to each other*

m a t r i m o n i a l

very culture has its own fads about best positions, and experiment is essential. If we come back to the good old Adam and Eve missionary position with him on top, astride or between, and her underneath facing – and we do come back to it – that is because it's uniquely satisfying. Chiefly it's unique in its adaptability to mood; it can be wildly tough or very tender, long or quick, deep or shallow.

Matrimonial is the starting point for nearly every sequence, second only to the side positions, and the most reliable mutual finishing-point for orgasm. If you start in it you can deepen it by raising her legs, move to the clitoris by putting one leg between hers, roll about or right over, finishing with her on top, kneel and lie back into the Letter X with each partner lying between the

matrimonial *Uniquely satisfying in its adaptability to mood and the ideal quick-orgasm position*

19

other's legs (see *x position*), move into back, side or standing positions, then come back for the finish. Even excluding leg-raising variants this position has won more medals at international expositions than any other.

The tuning adjustments for matrimonials can be highly important – hard enough bed, use of pillows if she is slim. Tough or tender, how high you ride, pinned down or not pinned down, astride her legs or between them, spreading her with your legs – all make subtle differences.

The Missionary position is the name given by amused Polynesians, who preferred squatting intercourse, to the European matrimonial.

postures *The variety of possible ways of having intercourse is an ancient fascination, and a great way of finding out what each of you likes*

u p p e r   h a n d s

f the matrimonial is the king of postures, the queen is her turn on top, 'riding St George'. Indian erotology is the only ancient tradition devoid of stupid patriarchal hang ups about the need for her to be underneath, and unashamed about accepting her fully aggressive role in reciprocal sex.

With a woman who has good vaginal muscle control it can be fantastic for the man, but for her it is unique, giving her total freedom to control movement, depth and her partner.

She can lean forward for breast or mouth kisses, back to show herself to him, touch her own clitoris as she moves, delay if she wishes, for emphasis – the lot. She can ride him facing or facing away, or turn from one into the other.

upper hands *For her it is a unique position, giving her total freedom to control movement and her partner*

f r o n t a l

All the face-to-face positions where one
partner has both thighs between those of
the other – he astride both hers or between them.
Includes all the varieties of the *matrimonial* plus
most of the more complicated, deep
facing positions. Gives more depth
(usually) but less clitoral pressure than
the *flanquettes*. To unscramble a
complicated posture for purposes of
classification, turn the partners
round mentally and see if they
can finish up face-to-face in a
matrimonial without crossing
legs. If so, it's frontal. If not,
and they finish face-to-face
astride one leg, it's *flanquette*;

square from behind (*croupade*); or from behind, astride a leg (*cuissade*). It's as simple as that.

Postures are to be used in sequence and one needs to make as few radical shifts as possible. Whichever partner leads needs to envisage all the stages in getting where they are going to avoid clumsiness and breaks, other than natural and intended ones.

frontal *Not one, but a range of positions for deep penetration*

i n v e r s i o n

N ot homosexuality, which isn't in our book, but taking him or her head-down. He can sit on a chair or stool and take her astride facing – then she lies back until her head rests on a cushion on the floor. Or she can lie down, raising her hips – he stands between her legs and enters her either from in front or from behind while she rests on her elbows or walks on her hands (the *wheelbarrow*). He can lie over the edge of the bed, face up, while she sits or stands astride. With orgasm the buildup of pressure in the veins of the face and neck can produce startling sensations.

Unless you want a body on your hands, better not try this on a hypertensive executive – remember Attila the Hun's young concubine – but it should be safe enough for youngsters. It is the way to handle those idiotic people who try to persuade a lover to boost their orgasm by throttling them – if you meet one of these, never do anything so damned silly, but teach them this alternative and equally rewarding method. You may save two lives – hers, and, since most people's grip tightens in orgasm, her next boyfriend's, which could easily be spent in jail for homicide.

A variation on the inverted position is 'inverted 69' – mutual oral intercourse. This always works if you can lift her, and will give her an idea of the quality of sensation involved; not everyone likes it.

inversion *For the young and fit – a safer alternative to strangulation*

f l a n q u e t t e

he half-facing group of sexual postures – she lies facing
him with one of her legs between his, and consequently one
of his legs between hers, the frontal equivalent of the *cuissades*.
These positions give extra clitoral pressure from the man's thigh if
he presses hard with it.

semi-facing positions *can stimulate
her more than straight matrimonial*

flanquette *Half-facing, with the*
possibility of extra clitoral pressure

x position

A *winner for prolonged slow intercourse.* Start with her sitting facing astride him, penis fully inserted. She then lies right back until each partner's head and trunk are between the other's wide-open legs, and they clasp hands. Slow, coordinated wriggling movements will keep him erect and her close to orgasm for long periods. To switch back to other positions, either of them can sit up without disconnecting.

31

x position *For slow, drawn-out intercourse, this is a winner*

s t a n d i n g p o s i t i o n s

The traditional upright is a quickie, and apt to produce stiff male muscles unless she is tall. Many women need to stand on two phone directories with the yellow pages, or an equivalent. Best undertaken up against a solid object such as a wall or a tree (not a door, whichever way it opens). Alternatively, you can be free standing, legs apart for stability and arms

standing positions *If your relative heights and her weight permit, this variant extends coition for both partners*

clasped around each other's buttocks – looking down as you move can be really sensual.

There are two kinds of position – this one, subject to a good match in height, and the Hindu versions where he picks her up; these are tremendous if she is light as an Oriya dancing girl, otherwise they need to be executed in water to make her weightless.

standing positions *This is subject to a good match in height and is an ideal position for quickies*

rear entry

T*he other human option* – for most mammals it's the only one.

The lack of face-to-faceness is more than compensated for by extra depth and buttock stimulation, hand access to breasts and clitoris, and the sight of a pretty rear view. For the standing positions she needs something of the right height to support her – in the head-down kneeling positions you need to be careful not to push her face into the mattress, and in all of the deep variants you need to avoid going too deep too hard, or you will hit an ovary, which is as painful as hitting a testicle. A few woman are put off by the symbolism – 'doing it like animals' – but the physical pay-off is so intense for both participants that they shouldn't allow these feelings to make them miss it.

rear entry *All the rear entry positions*
give greater depth of penetration

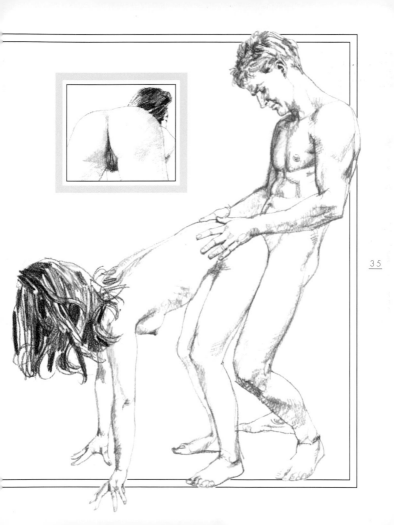

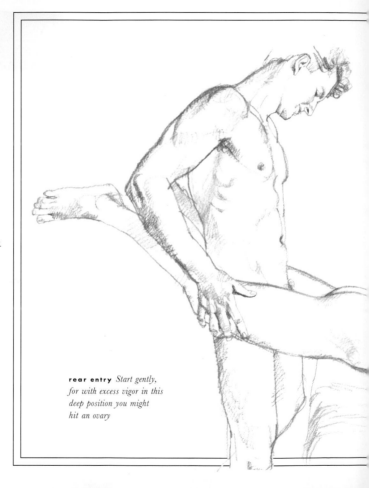

36

rear entry *Start gently,
for with excess vigor in this
deep position you might
hit an ovary*

head down

T he head-down position is best for depth or total apposition –
avoid it if it hurts her, or if she has a weak back, or if she is
pregnant. While the deep kneeling position is, or can be, one of
the toughest, from behind on your sides is about the gentlest
and can even be done in
sleep. It's well worth
experimenting with the
full range of rear
positions because there
will be at least one
you'll almost certainly use
regularly along with the
matrimonial and its
variants and the
woman-astride
positions.

*n*égresse

À *la négresse* – from behind. She kneels, hands clasped behind her neck, breasts and face on the bed. He kneels behind. She hooks her legs over his and pulls him to her with them – he puts a hand on each of her shoulder-blades and presses down. Very deep position – apt to pump her full of air which escapes later in a disconcerting matter – otherwise excellent.

négresse *Very deep position, take care not to push her face into the mattress*

c r o u p a d e

A*ny position* in which he takes her squarely from behind, *ie*
all rear-entry positions except those where she has one
leg between his or is half-turned on her side (see *cuissade*).

41

croupade *Squarely from behind*

c u i s s a d e

T*he half-rear entry positions,* where she turns her back to him and he enters with one of her legs between his and the other more or less drawn up: in some versions she lies half-turned on her side for him, still facing away.

cuissade *Half-rear, half-side entry*

f l o r e n t i n e

Coitus à la florentine: intercourse with the woman holding the man's penile skin (and foreskin if he has one) forcibly back with finger and thumb at the root of the penis and keeping it stretched all the time, both in and out. Excellent way of speeding up ejaculation, and greatly boosts intensity of the male sensation if you get the tension right.

florentine *Intense sensations for him, and a quick finish*

saxonus *Interrupting ejaculation to prolong his peak*

46

s a x o n u s

oitus saxonus – pressing firmly on the male urethra near
the root of the penis to prevent ejaculation and (hope-
fully) conception. No use as a contraceptive, since sperm are
around long before he ejaculates – but some women do have the
knack, during masturbation, of stopping and restarting ejaculation by urethral pressure so as to spin out the male peak.

This is best done by pressing on the shaft near the root with
two or three fingers, but you need to press hard (don't bruise).
Some people press midway between scrotum and anus. The
idea is to allow ejaculation to occur piecemeal. If you stop it alto-
gether, he will eventually ejaculate into the bladder. There's no
evidence that this is harmful unless done violently and often, but
it's better avoided. Interrupting ejaculation is probably harmless
but it won't work on everyone. Women who have this party piece
say it is appreciated, but that may depend on their partner. You
might as well stop just short of ejaculation, then start again.

p o m p o i r

*T*he *most sought-after* feminine sexual response of all. 'She must . . . close and constrict the Yoni until it holds the Lingam as with a finger, opening and shutting at her pleasure, and finally acting as the hand of the Gopala-girl who milks the cow. This can be learned only by long practice, and especially by throwing the will into the part affected . . . Her husband will then value her above all women, nor would he exchange her for the most beautiful queen in the Three Worlds . . . Among some races the constrictor vaginae muscles are abnormally developed. In Abyssinia, for instance, a woman can so exert them as to cause pain to a man, and, when sitting on his thighs, she can induce orgasm without moving any other part of her person. Such an artist is called by the Arabs Kabbazah, literally, a holder, and it is not surprising that slave dealers pay large sums for her.'

Thus Richard Burton. It has nothing to do with 'race' but a lot to do with practice.

pompoir *Acquiring the knack of contracting and relaxing her vaginal muscles takes a lot of practice*

49

b i r d s o n g   a t   m o r n i n g

What your partner says in orgasm should never be quoted at him or her – it can only be played back when you are both in a suitable mood. There is a striking consistency in what women say in orgasm. They babble about dying, about mother and about religion. This is natural – orgasm is the most religious moment of our lives. Men are apt to growl like bears, or utter aggressive monosyllables like 'In, In, In!'

It's hard to say why these cries are so charming in both sexes. It is important to learn how to read them and in particular to know when 'stop' means stop and when it means 'for God's sake let's go on.' The point is this: in mutual, let-go intercourse, make as much noise as you like.

birdsong at morning *Letting go completely, people can say strange things, don't bring these up the next morning*

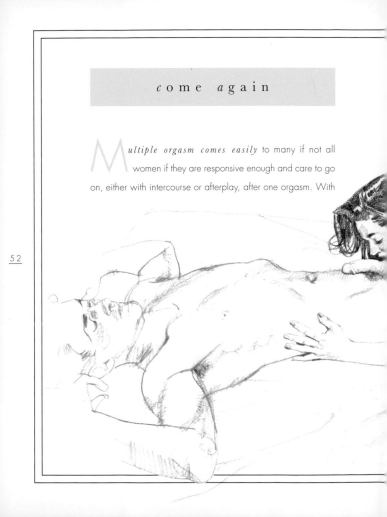

c o m e   a g a i n

Multiple orgasm comes easily to many if not all women if they are responsive enough and care to go on, either with intercourse or afterplay, after one orgasm. With men it is more complicated. Some can get six or more full orgasms in a few hours provided they aren't timestressed and don't attempt it daily. Some can do it daily. Others can't get a second erection for a set time. In any case it's not, for the man, the number of orgasms that matter, it is rather the ability either to hold off your own orgasm as long as you want, or to go on after, or soon after it, even if you don't come a second time.

come again *Waking the dead*

A bility to hold and to repeat is particularly important to the many (usually over-continent) males who have hair-trigger (premature ejaculation) trouble. It matters not a jot provided you can get another erection inside half an hour. If he can't, doesn't, or is worried about it, it is no use reasoning with him. You, Madam, must take over. Suggest some diversionary entertainment, give him half an hour, then stiffen him yourself by hand- or mouthwork. Tell him out of hours what you intend doing; you want to see how soon he can get stiff again. Bring this off neatly and you'll have added a new dimension to both your lives.

hair-trigger trouble
She should be sparing with very stimulating techniques ahead of penetration

l i t t l e d e a t h

a petite mort: some women do indeed pass right out, the 'little death' of French poetry. Men occasionally do the same. The experience is not unpleasant, but it can scare an inexperienced partner cold. A friend of ours had this happen with the first girl he ever slept with. On recovery she explained, 'I'm awfully sorry, but I always do that.' By then he had called the police and the ambulance. So there is no cause for alarm, any more than over the yells or sobbing, or any of the other unexpected reactions which go with complete orgasm in some people. By contrast others simply shut their eyes, but enjoy it no less. Sound and fury can be a flattering testimonial to a partner's skills, but a fallacious one, because they don't depend on the intensity of feeling, nor it upon them. Men don't often pass right out — that's her privilege, though they can give a splendid impersonation of a fit. In any case you'll soon get to know your partner's pattern once you're past any initial shocks.

south slav style

*W*ell *documented* because of the very rich erotic folksong repertoire of the region that became the former Yugoslavia. Intercourse naked, with emphasis on the importance to both of you of the genital perfume.

There are several reputedly 'national' positions or approaches. Serbian intercourse (*Srpski jeb*) is mock rape – you throw her down, seize one ankle in each hand and raise them over her head, then enter her with your full weight. Croatian intercourse (*Hrvatski jeb*) is a woman's ploy – an elaborate tongue bath, with the man free or staked out, followed after leisurely stimulation by riding him astride. The *Lion* position is a male masturbation method – squat down, heels to scrotum, place the penis between your ankles, rest on buttocks and hands, and move legs together.

57

south slav style
*It's vigorous
and no-nonsense,
but does not
lack warmth*

chinese style

In the classical treatises, remarkably like uninhibited European sex, the best thing being the delightful names given to postures: 'Wailing Monkey Clasping a Tree,' 'Wild Geese Flying on their Backs,' for two quite ordinary positions (seated face to face; woman on top facing away). The main elaboration consists in various complicated mixtures of deep and shallow strokes, often in magical numbers – 5 deep, 8 shallow, and so on. Intercourse is performed naked, on a Chinese bed, in the open air, or on the floor and the woman treated far less as an equal in sex than in Indian erotology.

chinese style *As in Indian erotology, mystery and magic play roles in Chinese sexual literature and practice*

j a p a n e s e   s t y l e

ntercourse on the floor or on cushions, as with most oriental styles: partial nakedness only, numerous squatting and semi-squatting positions, a lot of bondage, a lot of preoccupation with extras and odd devices. We're talking here about the sexual customs known from eighteenth- and early nineteenth-century prints, rather than the modern westernized B-girl version.

What would be hard to copy is the essentially Japanese mixture of violence and formality, which does not sit easily with our tradition of tenderness. Other differences are: elaborate finger-stimulation of the woman, thumb in anus, fingers in vagina: and a big range of mechanical devices – a glanscap of hard material (*kabutogata*), penile-shaft tubes (*do-gata*), some of them latticed (*yoroi-gata*), or with a glanscap as well (*yaso—gata*), dildoes (*engi*), often strapped to the woman's heel, while her ankle is held up to a sling round her neck to give a better swing to the movement; thongs to bind tightly round the penile shaft, rendering it both rough and permanently stiff enough for insertion (*higozuiki*), and merkins to hold in the hand (*azuma-gata*).

Postures cover the whole range, but the lovers of the 'floating world' greatly enjoy the simulation of rape – what George Moore called 'furious fornications' – where the artistic emphasis is on huge parts, copious secretions and so on: sex is played hard in this tradition.

japanese style *Traditional Japanese practice includes finger-stimulation of the woman*

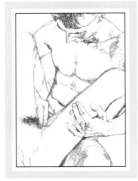

indian style

*N*ow *widely familiar* from the *Kama Sutra*, the *Koka Shastra*, etc. Intercourse on a bed or on cushions, fully naked, but with the woman wearing all her ornaments. Many complicated positions, including some derived from yoga which aim to avoid ejaculation, standing positions, and woman-on-top positions (*purushayita*) which are regarded as specially devout, since in Tantric Hinduism she is Energy and he is Immanence. All intimately linked with the Indian love of living at several levels – not only sex, but meditative technique in which one attempts to be both male and female for mystical purposes, or modified dance in which beside making love one acts out a scene from the hagiography of Vishnu and his Avatars, or the Life of the Rama.

Specialities include love-cries (see *Birdsong at morning*), love-blows (struck with fingertips on one another's breast, back, buttocks and genitals), lovebites as tokens of possession, and erotic scratchmarks.

f all the Indian techniques the standing postures are probably the best worth learning, if the girl is light enough. Few women who weren't trained from birth could stand leaning backwards on feet and hands, limbo-style, then put their arms round their legs and their head between their thighs, so as to take alternate strokes in mouth and vagina – or manage the one-leg-standing, one-leg-around-waist poses cultivated by temple girls.

indian style *This includes an amazing variety of positions and a certain degree of suppleness*